THE
NBA
A HISTORY OF HOOPS

Published by Creative Education
P.O. Box 227, Mankato, Minnesota 56002
Creative Education is an imprint of The Creative Company
www.thecreativecompany.us

Design and production by Christine Vanderbeek
Art direction by Rita Marshall

Printed by Corporate Graphics in the United States of America

Photographs by Dreamstime (Munktcu), Getty Images (Andrew D. Bernstein/
NBAE, Nathaniel S. Butler/NBAE, Sam Greenwood, Jon Hayt/NBAE, Tim
Heitman/NBAE, Yale Joel/Time & Life Pictures, Chris McGrath, Fernando
Medina/NBAE, Doug Pensinger, Tony Ranze/AFP, SM/AIUEO, Matt
Stroshane, Noren Trotman/NBAE), iStockphoto (Brandon Laufenberg)

Library of Congress Cataloging-in-Publication Data
Dittmer, Lori.
The story of the Orlando Magic / by Lori Dittmer.
p. cm. — (The NBA: a history of hoops)
Includes index.
Summary: The history of the Orlando Magic professional basketball
team from its start in 1989 to today, spotlighting the franchise's
greatest players and reliving its most dramatic moments.
ISBN 978-1-58341-956-4
1. Orlando Magic (Basketball team)—History—Juvenile literature.
2. Basketball—Florida—Orlando—History—Juvenile literature. I. Title. II. Series.
GV885.52.O75D48 2009   796.323'640975924—dc22   2009035972

CPSIA: 120109 PO1093

First Edition
2 4 6 8 9 7 5 3 1

Page 3: Forward Brandon Bass
Pages 4–5: Guard Penny Hardaway

THE STORY OF THE
ORLANDO MAGIC

LORI DITTMER

CREATIVE ● EDUCATION

CONTENTS

CHAPTER ONE

MAKING THE MAGIC

Orlando, Florida, was originally called Jernigan in the 1840s, after the family that first settled there. The city's name was changed to Orlando during the 1850s. History does not clearly explain the change, but one theory holds that the city was renamed in honor of Orlando Reeves, an American soldier who was killed during the Seminole Wars of the early 1800s. In the century and a half since, the community's warm weather and tourist attractions have made it one of the most popular vacation destinations in the United States.

Orlando's biggest attraction is the nearby Walt Disney World Resort, which includes Epcot and the Magic Kingdom. Yet this central Florida city is also home to another kind of Magic—the Orlando Magic, a professional basketball team that has been entertaining fans since the franchise was born as a new member of the National Basketball Association (NBA) in 1989.

In 1986, a group of investors led by Orlando businessman Jim Hewitt and former Philadelphia 76ers general manager Pat Williams began lobbying the NBA to create a new franchise

Epcot, which opened in 1982, helps make the Orlando area a tourism hotspot, welcoming more than 10 million visitors every year.

DURING THE MID-1980S, THE NBA DECIDED TO EXPAND ITS 23-TEAM LEAGUE BY 3 FRANCHISES. In April 1987, the NBA Board of Governors granted Charlotte, North Carolina, a franchise to begin play in 1988 and Minneapolis, Minnesota, another to start up the following season. Two Florida cities—Orlando and Miami—were vying for the third franchise. However, unable to choose just one, the committee accepted both into the NBA. The Miami Heat joined the league in 1988, and the Magic entered the next year. As they became a part of the league, the new teams rotated through the NBA's divisions. Orlando, despite its southern location, began as part of the Eastern Conference's Central Division. The team then moved into the Midwest Division and finally settled into the Atlantic Division for the 1991–92 season. "This rotating system will give the fans in these new franchise cities a chance to see all the NBA stars several times in the first three years," said league commissioner David Stern. When the teams at last migrated into their permanent geographic divisions, he said, they could "build rivalries with existing teams in the same area."

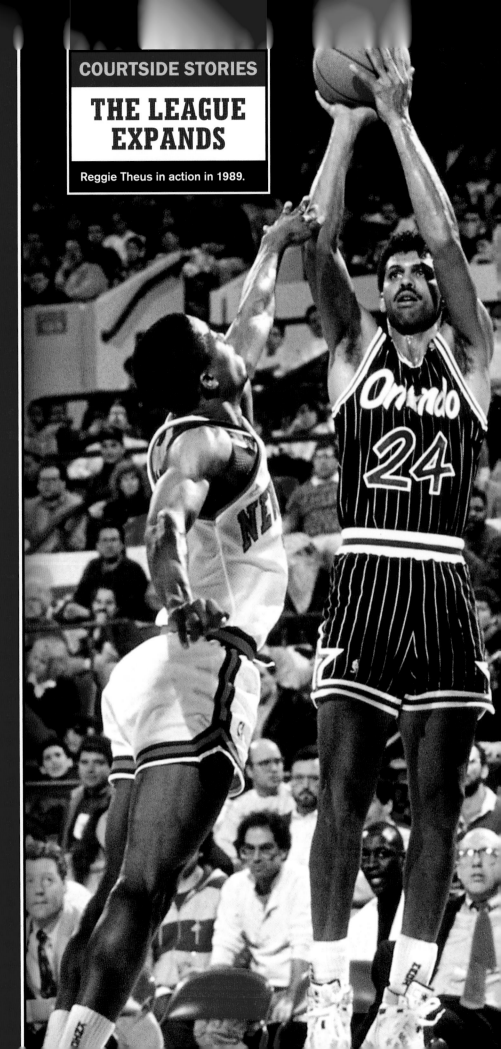

COURTSIDE STORIES

THE LEAGUE EXPANDS

Reggie Theus in action in 1989.

in Orlando. The group won the league over and earned that franchise in 1987, and a year later, Williams hired former 76ers coach Matt Guokas as the Magic's first head coach. "The opportunity to build something in two, three, four, five years is something I thought might be fun," Guokas said.

Orlando's first roster was built primarily through an expansion draft in which the Magic, as well as the newly formed Minnesota Timberwolves, were allowed to select players from most of the other existing NBA teams (the Charlotte Hornets and Miami Heat, which had entered the league the previous year, were exempt). Each existing team could protect its eight top players, which meant the expansion teams were generally left to select players who were backups or already past their prime. From this draft, the Magic acquired players such as slick-shooting guard Reggie Theus, forwards Terry Catledge and Sidney Green, and scrappy point guard Scott Skiles. Then, with the 11th overall pick in the 1989 NBA Draft, the Magic selected versatile University of Illinois swingman Nick Anderson as the first collegiate draft pick in team history.

The Magic thrilled a sold-out Orlando Arena during the team's first preseason game on October 13, 1989, defeating the defending world champion Detroit Pistons, 118–109. "We thought *we* were the defending

champions after that game," said Magic guard Morlon Wiley. The Magic
finished their first month in the NBA with a 7–7 record, the best start by
an expansion team in league history. After that, though, the team began
to falter. Despite Orlando's prolific offense, which ranked fifth in the
NBA in total points, the Magic were the league's worst club defensively.
Orlando ended its inaugural season 18–64.

With the fourth overall pick in the 1990 NBA Draft, the Magic
selected sharpshooter Dennis Scott, a forward from Georgia Tech.
Skiles improved his play during the 1990–91 season, reaching a
new level in December, when the veteran point guard set an NBA record
with 30 assists in a single game versus the Denver Nuggets. Skiles was
quick to share the credit. "If any of those shots were missed, I would
have fallen short, so I owe the record to my teammates," he said. The
Magic's teamwork paid off, and Orlando jumped to 31–51.

The team slipped to 21–61 the following season, but fans still turned
out to show their support, selling out all 41 home games. Despite all the
losses, there was a silver lining. The Magic's poor record put Orlando in
position to make an addition that would dramatically brighten the future
of the franchise.

INTRODUCING...

SCOTT SKILES

POSITION GUARD
HEIGHT 6-FOOT-1
MAGIC SEASONS 1989–94

THE MAGIC SELECTED SCOTT SKILES FROM THE INDIANA PACERS' ROSTER DURING THE NBA'S 1989 EXPANSION DRAFT. Known for his durability and gritty style of play, the point guard quickly became a fan favorite in Orlando, and during his Magic years, he was a nearly permanent fixture in every game. During the 1992–93 season, Skiles averaged 39 minutes played per game, second-most in the league. At 6-foot-1, Skiles was smaller than most NBA players, but he also played with greater intensity and self-confidence than most. "I played more of a tough kind of game," he said later, "but I had no choice. That was the only way I could play in order to survive and have a career." A team leader, Skiles poured his energy into motivating his teammates, which might be how he became the Magic's all-time leader in assists, with 2,776. In a victory over the Nuggets on December 30, 1990, he set a single-game NBA record with 30 assists. Skiles later became head coach of the Phoenix Suns, Chicago Bulls, and Milwaukee Bucks.

NICK ANDERSON EARNED AN HONORED PLACE IN

ORLANDO'S BASKETBALL STORY WHEN THE

FRANCHISE SELECTED HIM AS THE FIRST DRAFT

PICK (11TH OVERALL IN THE 1989 NBA DRAFT)

IN TEAM HISTORY. Entering the league out of the University of Illinois, Anderson was a versatile player who could swing between the forward and shooting guard positions. In both college and the pros, Anderson wore number 25 on his jersey in honor of Ben Wilson, a high school basketball teammate who was the victim of a senseless gang shooting. Over the course of 10 seasons in Orlando, Anderson accumulated several franchise records, including games played (692), career points (10,650), and steals (1,004). Although he wasn't as flashy or well-known as some of his Magic team-mates, Anderson shone when playing alongside the likes of center Shaquille O'Neal and guard Penny Hardaway. Anderson took advantage of being in the shadows of his peers. "When other teams key on them and forget about me," he said, "then there's the dagger, right in the heart." In 2006, Anderson rejoined the Magic as a community ambassador for the team.

CHAPTER TWO

THE O'NEAL ERA

The grand prize of the 1992 NBA Draft was Shaquille O'Neal, a 7-foot-1 and 300-pound center from Louisiana State University, whose rare combination of size and strength had scouts predicting instant stardom. All 11 teams that were eligible for the league's draft lottery, which determined the order in which non-playoff teams would select players, had prepared a jersey with O'Neal's name and number on it. On May 17, 1992, the NBA held the lottery, and with 10 chances out of 66, Orlando won the top pick and the young giant known as "Shaq."

In his first year, O'Neal averaged 23.4 points, 13.9 rebounds, and 3.5 blocked shots a game. "There's no doubt he's going to be a monster," said Miami Heat center Rony Seikaly. "He palms the ball like a grapefruit." Voted NBA Rookie of the Year, Shaq led the Magic to a respectable 41–41 mark, and Orlando missed the playoffs by the narrowest of margins. After the season, assistant coach Brian Hill was promoted to the head coaching position.

With his hustle and size, Shaquille O'Neal was a dominant offensive force from day one, scoring 46 points in one game as a rookie.

H aving assembled the best record among the league's non-playoff teams in 1992–93, the Magic had a scant 1-in-66 chance of obtaining the top pick in the 1993 Draft. Yet, unbelievably, Orlando won the number-one choice for the second year in a row. With it, the Magic chose brawny forward Chris Webber, then traded his rights to the Golden State Warriors for the rights to Memphis State University point guard Anfernee "Penny" Hardaway and three future first-round draft picks.

At 6-foot-7, Hardaway was taller than most point guards, yet he had the quickness and ball-handling ability to easily slash to the basket. With Hardaway and O'Neal, the Magic suddenly had one of the league's most potent and promising duos. "I'm glad I'm getting out of this game soon," said Los Angeles Lakers forward James Worthy. "I don't want to be around when those two grow up."

In 1993–94, O'Neal and Hardaway led the Magic to a 50–32 record, finishing second in the Eastern Conference's Atlantic Division. Although the Pacers swept the Magic in the first round of the playoffs, it was evident to all that Orlando was a team on the rise.

A BACKBOARD-BREAKING YEAR

A dunk-ravaged backboard.

DURING HIS FIRST YEAR IN THE NBA, CENTER SHAQUILLE O'NEAL ANNOUNCED HIS ARRIVAL BY DECLARING WAR ON THE LEAGUE'S BACKBOARDS. On February 7, 1993, Shaq slammed a ferocious dunk at America West Arena in Phoenix, then hung on the rim, pulling the backboard forward. The back end of the base lifted off the ground, and the collapsible basket folded into its storage position. The spectacle delayed the game 35 minutes while crews repaired the basket. Orlando lost the game 121–105, but O'Neal's dunk was the news of the night. Almost three months later in New Jersey, Shaq struck again with a power dunk in a game against the Nets. The dunk ripped apart the backboard's support braces; the backboard, stanchion, and base all had to be replaced, delaying the game for more than 45 minutes. Fortunately, the arena had an extra backboard to replace the broken pieces, and the Magic managed a 119–116 victory. "It really came crashing down," O'Neal said afterward. "The shot clock hit me in the head. It hurt a little bit, but not that much. I have a hard head."

AFTER LEAVING COLLEGE ONE YEAR EARLY TO ENTER THE 1990 NBA DRAFT, DENNIS SCOTT WAS SELECTED FOURTH OVERALL BY THE MAGIC, AND HE QUICKLY MADE HIS MARK. During his first NBA game, Scott drained three three-pointers in a three-minute span while wearing number three on his jersey—a debut performance that earned him the nickname "3-D." Scott's charismatic style and flashy smile earned him a large fan following, and he became known around the league for his long-distance shooting. "I just thank God every day for my personality and my jump shot," Scott once said. The forward went on to knock down 125 three-pointers during the 1990–91 season, which, at the time, was the best long-range production by a rookie in league history. Five years later, he made basketball history again when he finished the 1995–96 season with 267 three-pointers, an NBA single-season record that stood until 2006. When he was not playing basketball, the sharpshooter was talking about it. Scott enjoyed being in front of the camera, and during his time in Orlando, he hosted two television programs: "The Dennis Scott Show" and "The Highlight Zone."

One reason for the Magic's quick postseason knockout was the lack of a strong forward. In the off-season, Orlando added 6-foot-10 forward Horace Grant, a powerful defender who had won three NBA championships with the Chicago Bulls. Orlando also welcomed point guard Brian Shaw, formerly with the Heat. Shaw soon became half of the so-called "Shaw-Shaq Redemption," a crowd-pleasing, alley-oop pass play from Shaw to Shaq. When Scott sat out with a back injury, quick forward Donald Royal effectively filled in. The loaded 1994–95 Magic finished with a conference-best 57–25 mark. In the playoffs, the Magic powered past the Boston Celtics, Bulls, and Pacers to advance to the NBA Finals, where they faced star center Hakeem Olajuwon and the defending champion Houston Rockets. The Rockets were too much to handle, though, and they swept the Magic in four games.

The Magic returned with a vengeance in 1995–96. Orlando started 17–5, propelled in part by the long-range gunning of Scott, who set an NBA record with 267 three-pointers during the season. Orlando finished 60–22 and advanced to the Eastern Conference finals. But, facing the Bulls—who featured superstar guard Michael Jordan—Orlando was swept in four games.

COURTSIDE STORIES

THE ROAD TO THE FINALS

Guard Darrell Armstrong handles the ball during the 1995 Finals.

IN THE 1995 PLAYOFFS, THE FAST-RISING MAGIC SWEPT THE BOSTON CELTICS IN FOUR GAMES IN THE FIRST ROUND, THEN FACED THE CHICAGO BULLS. Orlando trailed the Bulls late in the fourth quarter of Game 1, when swingman Nick Anderson poked the ball away from Chicago guard Michael Jordan. Magic guard Penny Hardaway grabbed the loose ball, drove down the court, and passed to forward Horace Grant, who slammed home the game-winning basket with 6.2 seconds remaining. The Magic went on to clinch the series in six games. Next, Orlando faced the Pacers in the Eastern Conference finals, which went a full seven games. The Magic exploded in the third quarter of Game 7, pulling ahead by 19 points, and held on for the victory. In the NBA Finals, the Magic met the Rockets, who came back from a 20-point, second-quarter deficit in Game 1 to pull out a 120–118 overtime victory. The deflated Magic then lost the next three games in a series sweep. "It's a hard loss to take," center Shaquille O'Neal said. "I thought this was our year."

SHAQUILLE O'NEAL

AS A FRESHMAN AT LOUISIANA STATE UNIVERSITY, SHAQUILLE O'NEAL MEASURED 6-FOOT-11, BUT HE STILL WASN'T DONE GROWING. Three years later, he had added two more inches and won the Adolph Rupp trophy, presented to college basketball's top player. The NBA welcomed him via the 1992 Draft, where Orlando grabbed him with the top overall selection. Despite his imposing size, "Shaq" projected the image of a gentle giant, arriving for his new job in Orlando wearing Mickey Mouse ears. "He's a combination of the Terminator and Bambi," said O'Neal's agent, Leonard Armato. O'Neal was an instant success with the Magic, as well as in the commercial market, and throughout his career he acquired several nicknames, including "Big Diesel," which compared Shaq to a powerful engine, and "Big Aristotle," which referred to his commitment to sharp mental focus. His mere presence on the court was enough to change the game. Opponents usually double- or even triple-teamed O'Neal, leaving his teammates with more opportunities to score. After he left Orlando, O'Neal went on to win three NBA championships with the Lakers and one with the Heat.

CHAPTER THREE

HANDOFF TO HARDAWAY

Orlando fans were heartbroken when O'Neal left the Magic in the summer of 1996 to chase higher-profile stardom in Los Angeles with the Lakers. The team's fate now rested squarely on Hardaway's shoulders. "It's Penny's team now," said Grant, "and we'll go as far as he takes us."

Before the 1996–97 season, the Magic acquired veteran center Rony Seikaly—one of the best rebounders in the game—to help fill the void left by O'Neal. Although a knee injury sidelined Hardaway, Seikaly averaged 17.3 points and 9.5 boards a night to provide valuable offensive leadership. Late in the season, coach Brian Hill was fired and replaced by assistant Richie Adubato. The Magic finished 45–37, good enough for a spot in the playoffs.

A former member of the intrastate rival Miami Heat, center Rony Seikaly went from archenemy to fan favorite when he joined the Magic in 1996.

ORLANDO'S NBA FRANCHISE FOUND ITS NAME WITH THE HELP OF ITS FUTURE FANS, AS WELL AS THE INSPIRATION OF A LITTLE GIRL. While businessman Jim Hewitt and former 76ers general manager Pat Williams lobbied the NBA's expansion committee to bring professional basketball to Orlando, the *Orlando Sentinel* held a contest to name the team. A committee reviewed the 4,296 entries and selected 4 top possibilities: the Heat, Tropics, Juice, and Magic. Meanwhile, Williams's seven-year-old daughter, Karyn, visited him in Orlando. Together, they toured the Orlando area and its tourist attractions. When her trip was over, Karyn told her father, "I really like this place. This place is magic." Influenced by Karyn's comment, the naming committee whittled away the other potential names. Committee members decided that "Tropics" would better suit a southern Florida team rather than Orlando, a central Florida city. A recent hard winter had devastated the state's citrus industry, so the committee decided against "Juice." Finally, the committee ruled out "Heat," thinking the name carried a negative connotation. "Magic" was the remaining choice, and the committee agreed that the name represented the area well.

COURTSIDE STORIES

NAMING THE MAGIC

Cinderella Castle in the Walt Disney World Resort's Magic Kingdom.

n the first round of the postseason, Orlando faced off against the Heat, who crushed the Magic in the first two games. Orlando showed signs of life in Game 3 when 5-foot-11 point guard Darrell Armstrong—who had played a backup role during the regular season—sparked the team, scoring 21 points and allowing Hardaway to swing to the shooting guard spot. Hardaway poured in 42 points of his own, and the Magic took the game, 88–75. "It's one of the best performances I've ever seen Penny have since I've been here," said Adubato. Hardaway followed up that performance with 41 points in Game 4, leading Orlando to another victory. In Game 5, however, the Heat held on for a 91–83 win to take the game and the series.

Penny Hardaway's 1997 playoffs performance was one of his last true shining moments, as knee injuries would hinder his play soon after.

The next season, former Pistons coach Chuck Daly came to Orlando as the Magic's new bench leader. Injuries to Hardaway and Anderson crippled the team's title hopes in 1997–98, yet Armstrong and hard-working forwards Derek Strong and Charles "Bo" Outlaw still led the Magic to a respectable 41–41 finish.

In the 1998 NBA Draft, the Magic used two first-round selections to pick up bruising forward Matt Harpring and center Michael Doleac. Daly's second season as Orlando's coach was shortened to 50 games due to a dispute between NBA players and owners. After the 1998–99 season finally opened in February, the Magic bolted to a 33–17 record, then met the 76ers in the playoffs. The teams split the first two games, but star guard Allen Iverson led the 76ers to convincing victories in Games 3 and 4. "It's a big disappointment," Anderson said. "I thought we were a better team than this." After the season, Daly retired, and Hardaway asked to be traded.

In 1999, after Hardaway was sent to the Suns for two forwards—outside shooter Pat Garrity and savvy veteran Danny Manning—and two future first-round draft picks, the Magic hired former NBA guard Glenn "Doc" Rivers as their new head coach. Rivers's low-key style proved to be

the perfect tonic for the young Magic. With a roster devoid of big-name superstars (five players had not even been selected in the NBA Draft), Orlando was predicted by nearly every preseason publication to finish near the bottom of the league.

Yet during the season, the team adopted the slogan "Heart and Hustle," which described the group's hardworking and dedicated attitude. This determination helped the Magic to overachieve on almost every level. With Armstrong, Outlaw, smart center John Amaechi, and brawny forward Ben Wallace forming the core of the team, the Magic went 41–41, missing the playoffs by a single game. Rivers was then honored with the NBA Coach of the Year award, becoming just the fifth rookie head coach ever to claim the trophy.

ANFERNEE "PENNY" HARDAWAY

WHEN ANFERNEE HARDAWAY WAS A CHILD, HE LIVED WITH HIS GRANDMOTHER, WHO OFTEN CALLED HIM "PRETTY." With her thick Southern accent, the name sounded more like "Penny," and Hardaway's friends soon began calling him Penny, too. The third overall pick in the 1993 NBA Draft, Hardaway joined the Magic through a post-draft trade that sent

forward Chris Webber from Orlando to Golden State. Alongside superstar center Shaquille O'Neal, Hardaway became an instant sensation. As a rookie, he averaged 16 points per game and came in a close second to Webber in the Rookie of the Year award voting. Fans and coaches alike compared Hardaway to Lakers star Magic Johnson, as both were taller than most point guards yet

still excelled at handling the ball. Hardaway's unique combination of size and skill made him too big for most point guards to defend and too fast for many shooting guards to keep up with. "I can see why people compare him to Magic," said Orlando forward Dennis Scott. "He does whatever he feels the team needs, and that's what makes him the All-Star he is."

CHAPTER FOUR

TIME FOR T-MAC

The Magic made headlines in 2000 by signing both superstar forward Grant Hill and explosive swingman Tracy McGrady to free-agent contracts. Orlando then added another potent scorer by selecting 6-foot-8 guard/forward Mike Miller, known for his three-point-range marksmanship, with the fifth overall pick in the NBA Draft. "Last year, we built a nucleus of guys that work hard every night and do the little things," explained Coach Rivers. "Now, with the addition of Hill and McGrady, we have the weapons necessary to win the big games."

McGrady, known to fans as "T-Mac," made an immediate impact, scoring a career-high 32 points in the first game of the year. Hill, however, suffered from a lingering ankle injury, which kept him out of all but four games of the 2000–01 season. Despite Hill's absence, Rivers guided his young team to a 43–39 record. Miller set a new franchise record for the most three-pointers made by a rookie (148)—an achievement that helped him secure the 2001 NBA Rookie of the Year award. With McGrady averaging 26.8 points and 7.5 rebounds per game, the Magic made the playoffs for the sixth time in eight years.

Mike Miller led the University of Florida to college basketball's national championship game only months before the Magic drafted him in 2000.

Magic fans were left deflated as their team lost the first two games of an opening-round playoff series versus the Bucks. T-Mac gave them hope in Game 3, when he scored 42 points to boost Orlando to a 121–116 overtime victory. But the Magic could not hold on to that momentum, and the Bucks bounced Orlando out of the series in Game 4.

McGrady became a true NBA superstar the next season, as he and Lakers guard Kobe Bryant were the only two players in the league to average at least 25 points, 5 rebounds, and 5 assists per game. McGrady and the Magic played particularly well at home, going 27–14. His ankle still ailing, Hill missed all but 14 games, but with solid play from Grant, Armstrong, and Miller, the Magic finished 44–38. Orlando met Charlotte in the first round of the playoffs, but several Magic players were injured by season's end, and the team hobbled through the series (with McGrady taking breaks to lie on the floor to soothe his sore back), bowing to the Hornets in four games.

In 2002–03, two newcomers, sharpshooting guard Gordan Giricek and scrappy forward Drew Gooden, helped Orlando to finish 42–40—making it the 11th straight year in which the franchise finished .500 or better. The Magic faced the top-seeded Pistons in the Eastern

Although Tracy McGrady was best known for his scoring, his long wingspan and huge vertical leap made him a formidable defender as well.

Conference playoffs, and McGrady started the series with a bang, going for 43 and then 46 points in the first two games. But after capturing a three-games-to-one series lead, Orlando broke down. The Magic players began relying too heavily on McGrady, and the Pistons fought back to win the series in seven games. "I can't win it by myself," T-Mac said. "I'm pretty sure [my teammates] understand that."

Orlando began the 2003–04 campaign with an overtime win over the New York Knicks, but the season crumbled as the team lost the next 19 games. T-Mac continued to shine, setting a new franchise record with a 62-point game in a March win over the Washington Wizards. During the season, McGrady became the second-youngest player (after Kobe Bryant) in NBA history to reach 10,000 career points. Despite these highlights, Orlando plummeted to a 21–61 record, the worst in the league.

Frustrated by the poor season and the team's continuing playoff struggles, McGrady then asked to be traded. Orlando sent him, along with veteran forward Juwan Howard, to the Houston Rockets for quick guard Steve Francis, and the Magic embarked on another rebuilding project.

AID $300 FOR THIS SIGN, SO LEASE MAKE SOME **NOISE!**

STUFF, THE MAGIC MASCOT

Stuff fires up the home crowd.

EVEN BEFORE THE MAGIC PLAYED THEIR FIRST GAME, ORLANDO'S MASCOT—STUFF, THE MAGIC DRAGON—WAS BORN ... OR, MORE ACCURATELY, HATCHED. On October 27, 1988, a large egg appeared in front of the Magic's stadium, the Orlando Arena, or the "O-Rena." The egg exploded into a shower of deflated basketballs, bumper stickers, and puffs of green smoke. A tall, fuzzy green dragon with a pink-and-blue Mohawk and a five-foot wingspan emerged. Appropriately, Stuff made his community debut on Halloween that year at Church Street Station. Since then, Stuff has become one of the most recognizable mascots in professional sports. The dragon represents the Magic at every home game, and his antics and energy have earned him a large fan base of all ages. Stuff also attends Magic-related activities and civic and social events in central Florida. Stuff's favorite sayings include "Dragon my heels, but gotta fly" and "Stuff it!" To help entertain the crowds, Stuff enlists the help of two sidekicks, the inflatable Air Stuff and the small Mini Stuff, who occasionally appear with the original dragon.

CHAPTER FIVE

NEW MAGIC

Prior to the 2004–05 season, the Magic hit the lottery jackpot for the third time in franchise history, winning the top selection in the 2004 NBA Draft. With it, Orlando chose 6-foot-11 center Dwight Howard, a high school superstar from Atlanta, Georgia, who had earned the 2004 Naismith Award, given to the nation's top high-school player. The Magic also acquired rookie guard Jameer Nelson in a draft-night trade with the Nuggets. Before the start of the season, free-agent forwards Tony Battie and Turkish-born Hedo Turkoglu were also decked out in Orlando blue and white.

The retooled Magic started the season 13–7. The quick and confident Francis led the team with 21.3 points per game, while Hill, who had endured years of ankle pain and undergone several surgeries, finally returned to top form, averaging

Known both for his explosive scoring talent and his temperamental behavior, Steve Francis spent less than two full seasons in a Magic uniform.

19.7 points a night. Despite these efforts, the Magic finished the season a mere 36–46. Still, optimism was rising again in Orlando. "We've got something to look forward to next year," said Howard after the last game of the season.

Before the next season, Orlando brought back a familiar face as head coach—Brian Hill, who had led the Magic to 3 seasons of 50-plus wins in the 1990s. As the Magic started a disappointing 20–40 in 2005–06, the year's biggest highlight came from the 19-year-old Howard, who bounded into the NBA record books as the youngest player ever to notch a "20-20" game, with 21 points and 20 rebounds against the Charlotte Bobcats. The team pulled together to win 16 of its last 22 games to finish with the same record as the previous year.

Despite being ranked near the bottom of the league in turnovers, the Magic mustered a 40–42 mark in 2006–07. Orlando returned to the

Brian Hill built a distinguished record in his two stints as Orlando's bench leader, guiding the team to the playoffs in four of six seasons.

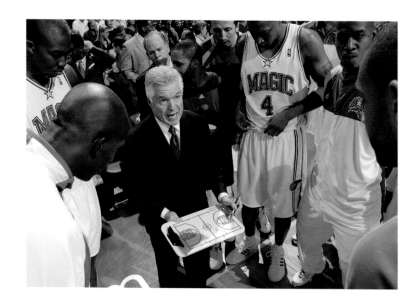

COURTSIDE STORIES

LOTTERY MAGIC

Dwight Howard with NBA commissioner David Stern at the 2004 Draft.

THE ANNUAL NBA DRAFT LOTTERY DETERMINES THE ORDER IN WHICH NON-PLAYOFF TEAMS GET TO DRAFT AMATEUR PLAYERS. During its first 20 years, Orlando beat the odds and won the number-one pick 3 times. In 1991–92, the Magic finished with the second-worst record in the league. The 11 teams with the worst marks were eligible for the lottery, which involved putting a total of 66 Ping-Pong balls in a drum. With 10 of the balls, the Magic had a 15.2 percent chance at the top pick. Orlando won the lottery and drafted center Shaquille O'Neal. The following year, the Magic just missed the playoffs. Having only one Ping-Pong ball in the 1993 lottery, they defied the odds to win the top spot again, then pulled a trade to acquire guard Anfernee "Penny" Hardaway. Orlando's third win came in 2004, when the team had the worst record and the most balls in the drum. "We suffered for every one of those balls," said Orlando general manager Pat Williams. "I'm just glad they did their job." With the top pick, the Magic selected high-school center Dwight Howard.

postseason for the first time in four years, but the Pistons made short work of the Magic, sweeping the series in four games. Shortly after that, Stan Van Gundy, a former coach of the Heat, took over as Orlando's head coach. The Magic then signed free-agent forward Rashard Lewis, an athletic and reliable scorer, from the Seattle SuperSonics.

The 2007–08 Magic vaulted to a 52–30 mark, Orlando's best since 1995–96. The record earned the team the third seed in the Eastern Conference playoffs. "We've had a good season," said Lewis, "but we know we have to win in the playoffs to get a little more respect." And win they did, defeating the Toronto Raptors in five games in the first round. Howard led the way, propelling his team as he posted at least 20 points and 20 rebounds in 3 games of the series. "To finally get over the hump and get out of the first round, it means a lot," said Howard. But the Pistons then ended the Magic's run, bouncing Orlando in the second round.

In the off-season, Orlando focused on placing new talent around its young center, signing versatile swingman Mickael Pietrus as a free agent and then nabbing Courtney Lee—a sweet-shooting guard out of Western Kentucky University—in the 2008 NBA Draft. The Magic started out hot in 2008–09, buoyed by Howard's first career triple-double—30 points, 19 re-

bounds, and 10 blocked shots—in a victory over the Oklahoma City Thunder. Nelson suffered a season-ending shoulder injury, and the Magic acquired speedy point guard Rafer Alston as a replacement.

Alston was just what Orlando needed to keep its playoff hopes alive, ensuring that the offense ran smoothly by getting the ball to prolific scorers such as Howard, Lewis, and Turkoglu. The Magic finished the season with their second-best record ever, 59–23, then embarked on a postseason run that opened eyes around the league. Orlando roared all the way to the NBA Finals by toppling the 76ers, the defending NBA champion Celtics, and the high-powered Cleveland Cavaliers, who were led by superstar forward LeBron James. The Magic could not quite reach the top of the mountain, though, losing to the Lakers in the Finals. A similar story played out in 2009–10. After adding All-Star swingman Vince Carter, the Magic again went 59–23, only to see their season end in the conference finals with a loss to the Celtics.

INTRODUCING...

DWIGHT HOWARD

POSITION CENTER
HEIGHT 6-FOOT-11
MAGIC SEASONS 2004–PRESENT

AS AN EIGHTH-GRADER, DWIGHT HOWARD SET A PERSONAL GOAL TO BECOME THE FIRST OVERALL SELECTION IN THE NBA DRAFT. After graduating from Southwest Atlanta Christian Academy in 2004, Howard fulfilled that goal and became the third player ever to be the top overall selection in the NBA Draft straight out of high school. The Magic immediately inserted him into the team's starting rotation, and the young center did not disappoint. With his size, speed, and power, Howard was one of only eight NBA players to average a double-double in 2004–05, netting 12 points and grabbing 10 rebounds per game. "He's just genetically superior to most people from a physical standpoint," said Orlando strength and conditioning coach Joe Rogowski. In addition to displaying his athleticism, Howard showed he was still a big kid during the 2008 All-Star Game weekend's Slam-Dunk Contest, when he captured first place while flying through the air wearing a Superman cape. In 2008, Howard said that during his first few years in the NBA, "the biggest thing was being on ESPN highlights. Now, it's seeing my team win."

For two decades, the Orlando Magic have been the model for building a successful NBA team from the ground up. Throughout poor seasons, lottery jackpots, and playoff berths, Orlando's fans have passionately supported the franchise. With the new roster of talent today rising up in central Florida, opponents might soon need a bit of magic themselves to stop Orlando.

With star swingman Vince Carter (opposite) playing alongside Rashard Lewis (below), the 2009–10 Magic remained an NBA power.

INDEX